Random Doodles

Volume 1

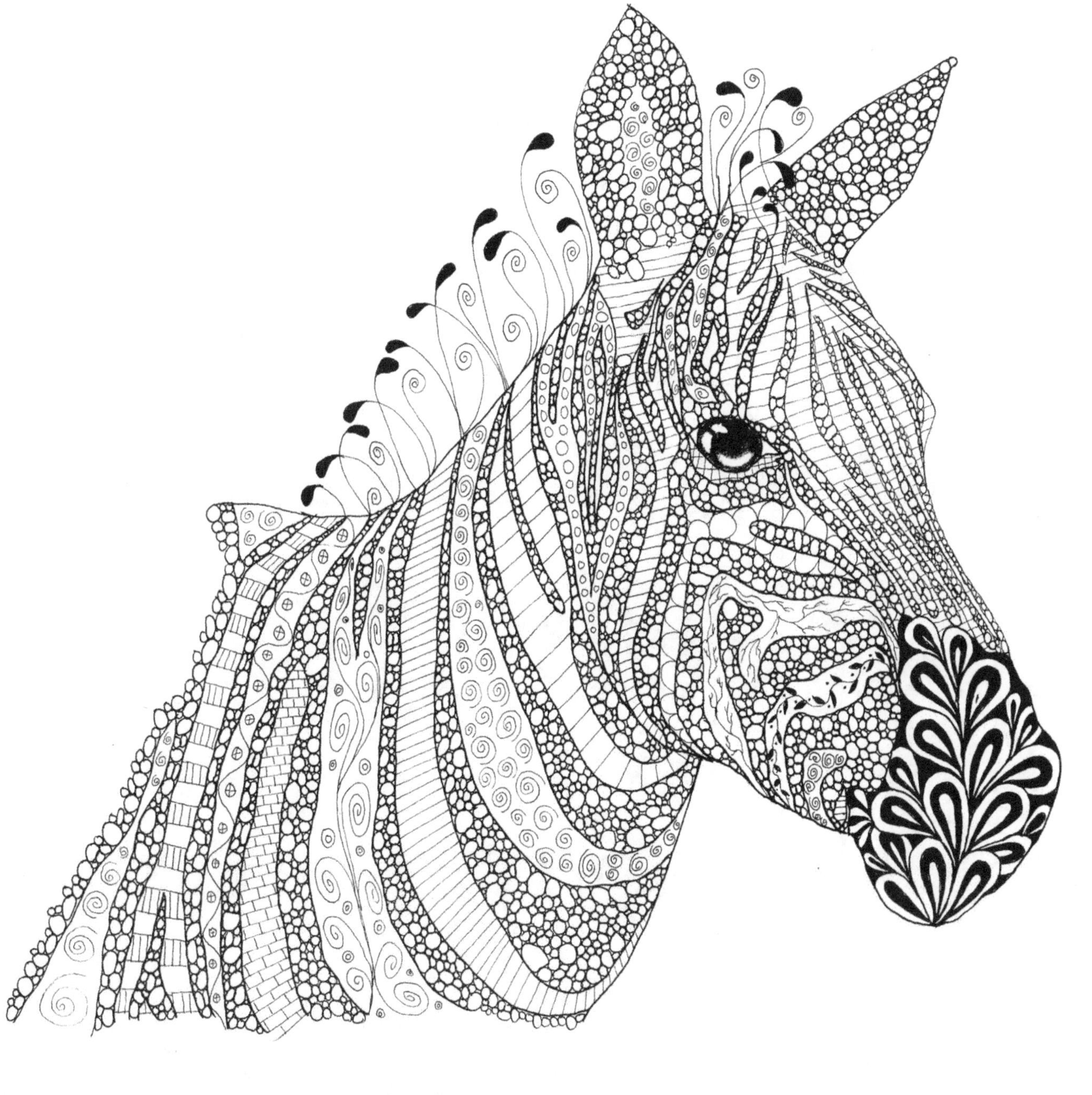

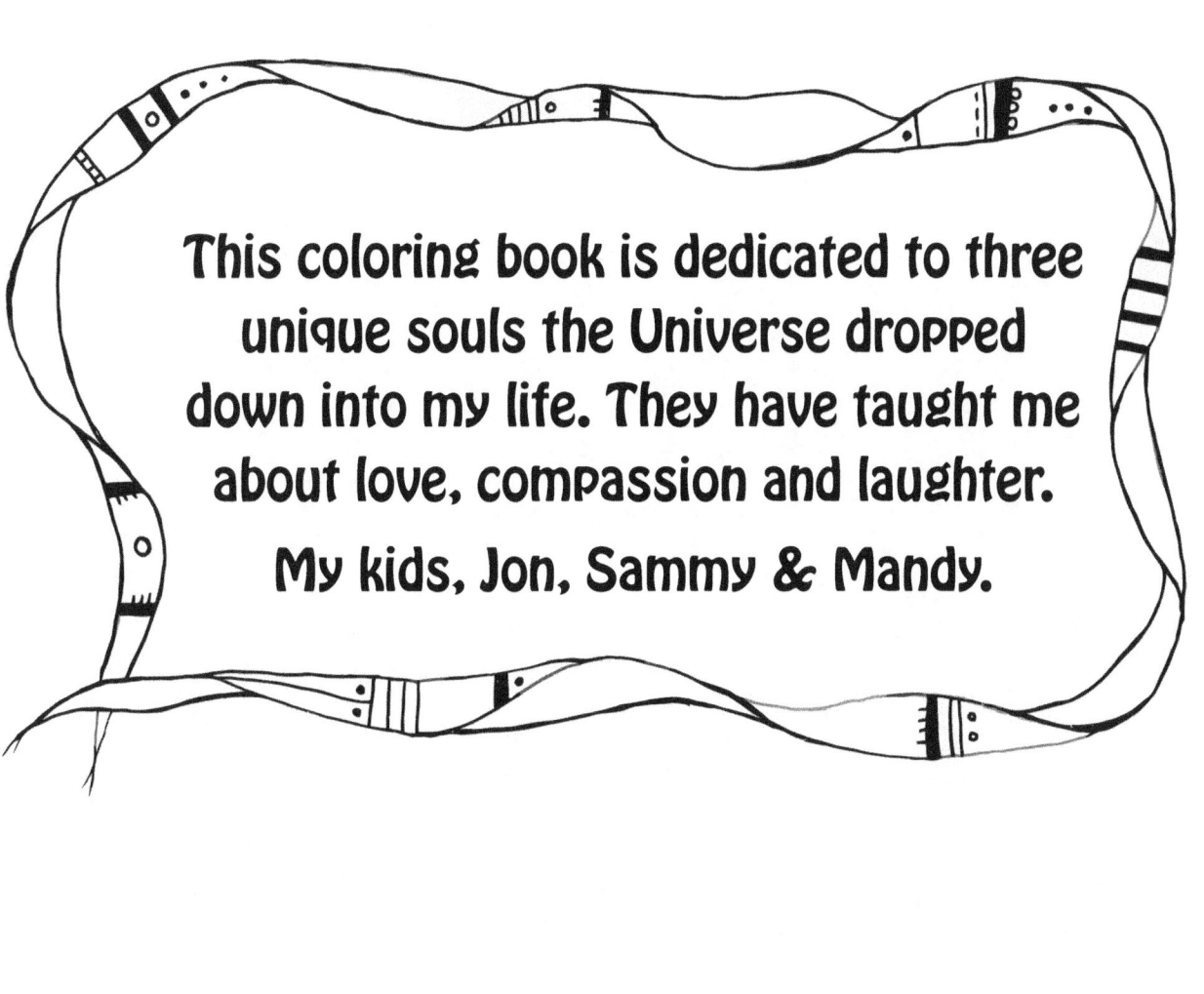

This coloring book is dedicated to three unique souls the Universe dropped down into my life. They have taught me about love, compassion and laughter.

My kids, Jon, Sammy & Mandy.

In the last few years adult coloring books have become best sellers on Amazon.com. There have been countless articles written on the therapeutic qualities of coloring. And most of us women are saying, "Heck yes, we've been coloring for years." I guess we just needed someone to tell us to quit hiding and color with pride. It's ok to color because we want to and quit pretending we are just coloring with our kids and grandkids.

The articles are right, it is relaxing and relieves tension and stress. It is a new form a meditation. Coloring is one of the healthiest ways to free your mind. Who doesn't need that in today's world?

Well, now you have permission. Color all you want! Color in the morning with your coffee, in the afternoon on your lunch break, or at night with a glass of wine. Just color!

Happy Coloring!

Peace, Love & Funk,

Sue

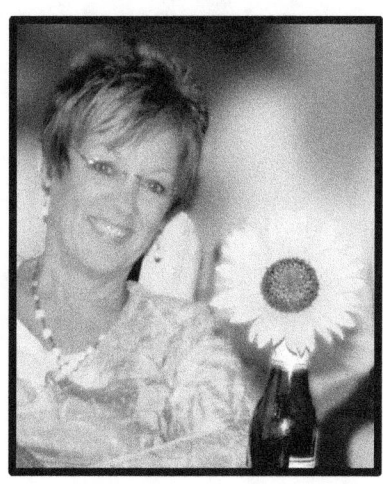

Be a lamp, or a lifeboat, or a ladder.

Help someone's soul heal.

Walk out of your house like a shepherd.

~ Rumi

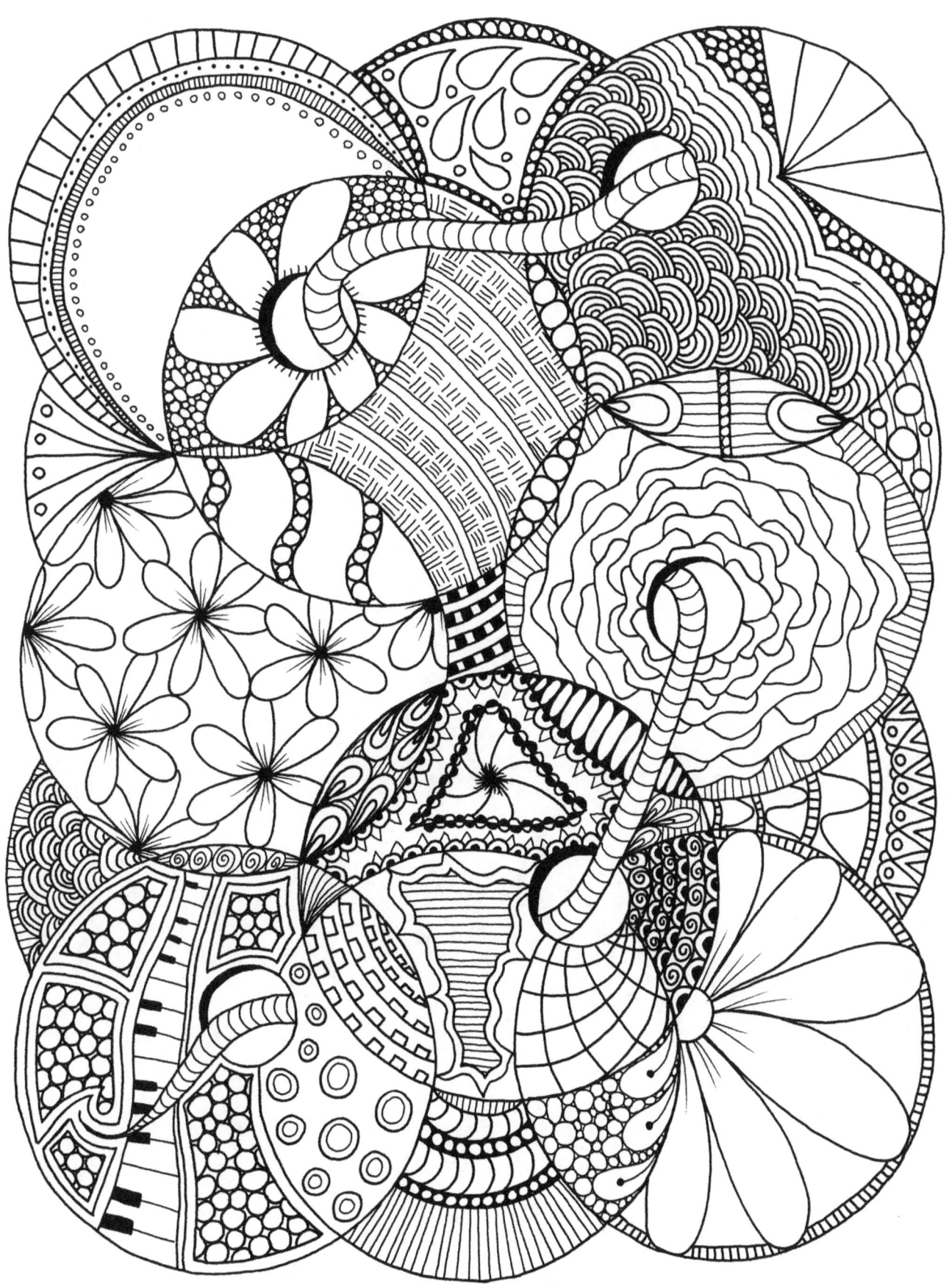

When I was 5 years old, my mother always told me that happiness was the key to life. When I went to school, they asked me what I wanted to be when I grew up. I wrote down 'happy'. They told me I didn't understand the assignment, and I told them they didn't understand life.
~ John Lennon

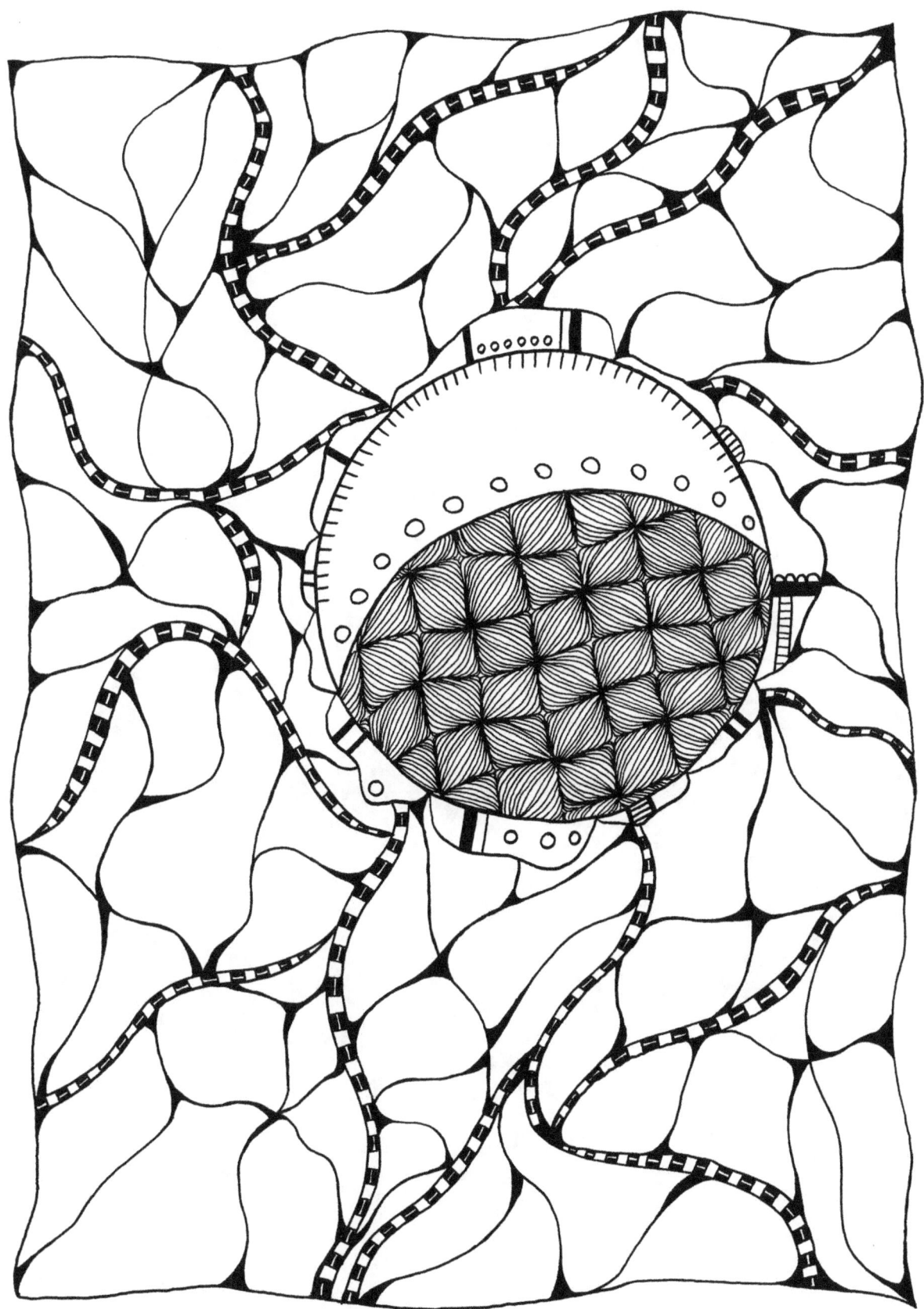

Peace. It does not mean to be in a place
where there is no noise, trouble, or hard work.
It means to be in the midst of those things
and still be calm in your heart.
~ Unknown

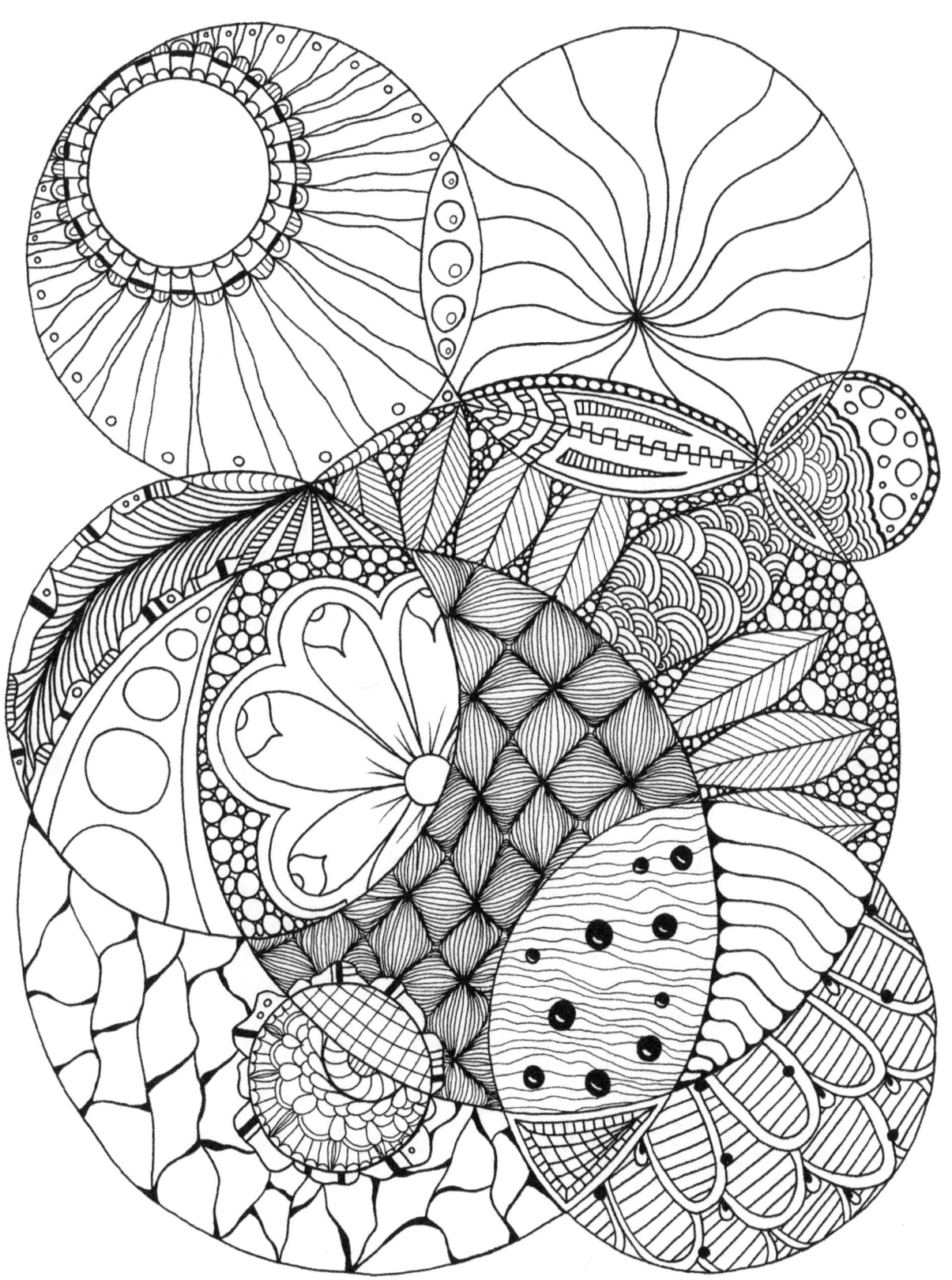

No one is useless in the world
who lightens the burden of it for anyone else.
~Charles Dickens

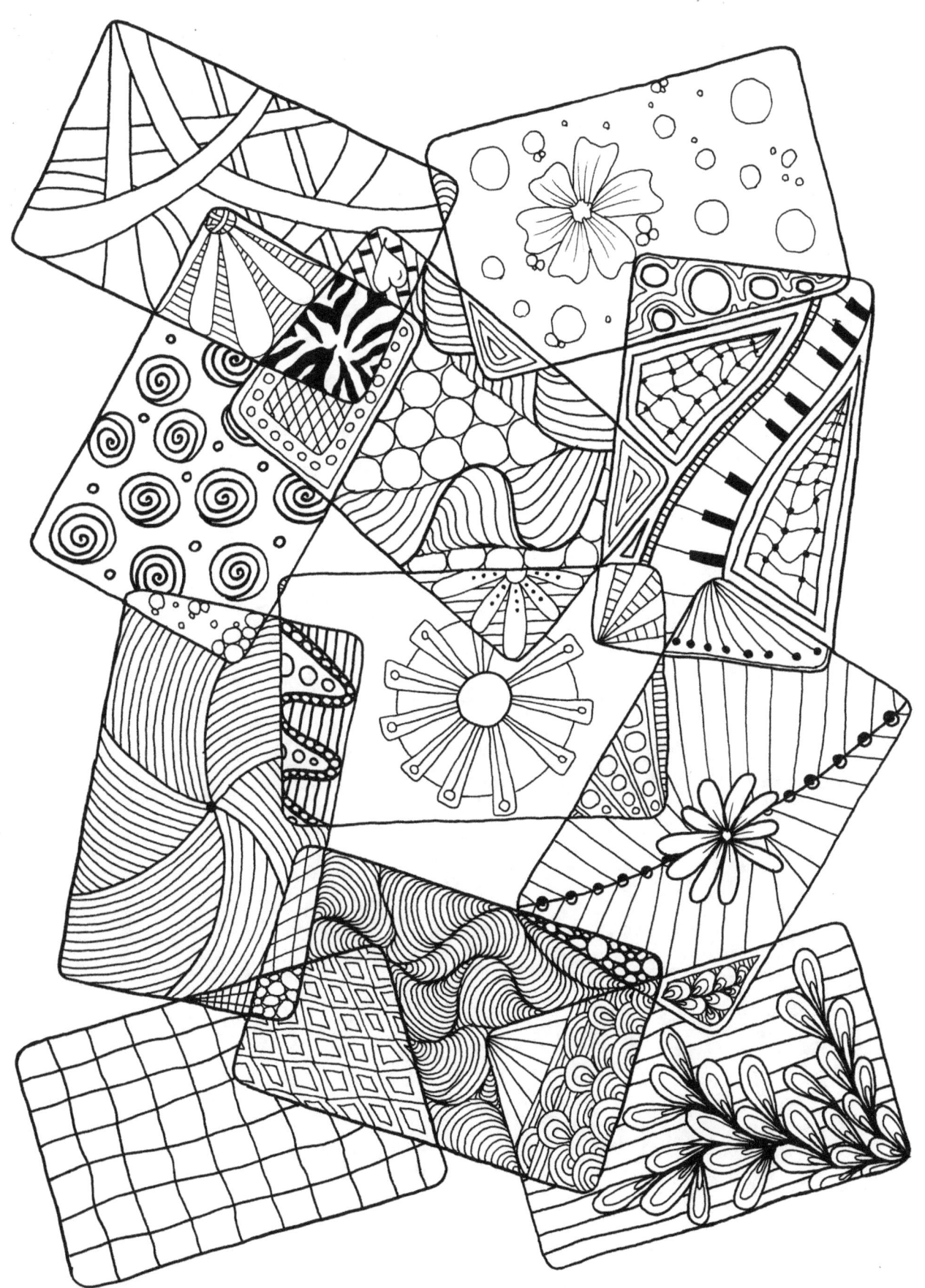

The best and most beautiful things in the world
cannot be seen or even touched -
they must be felt with the heart.
~ Helen Keller

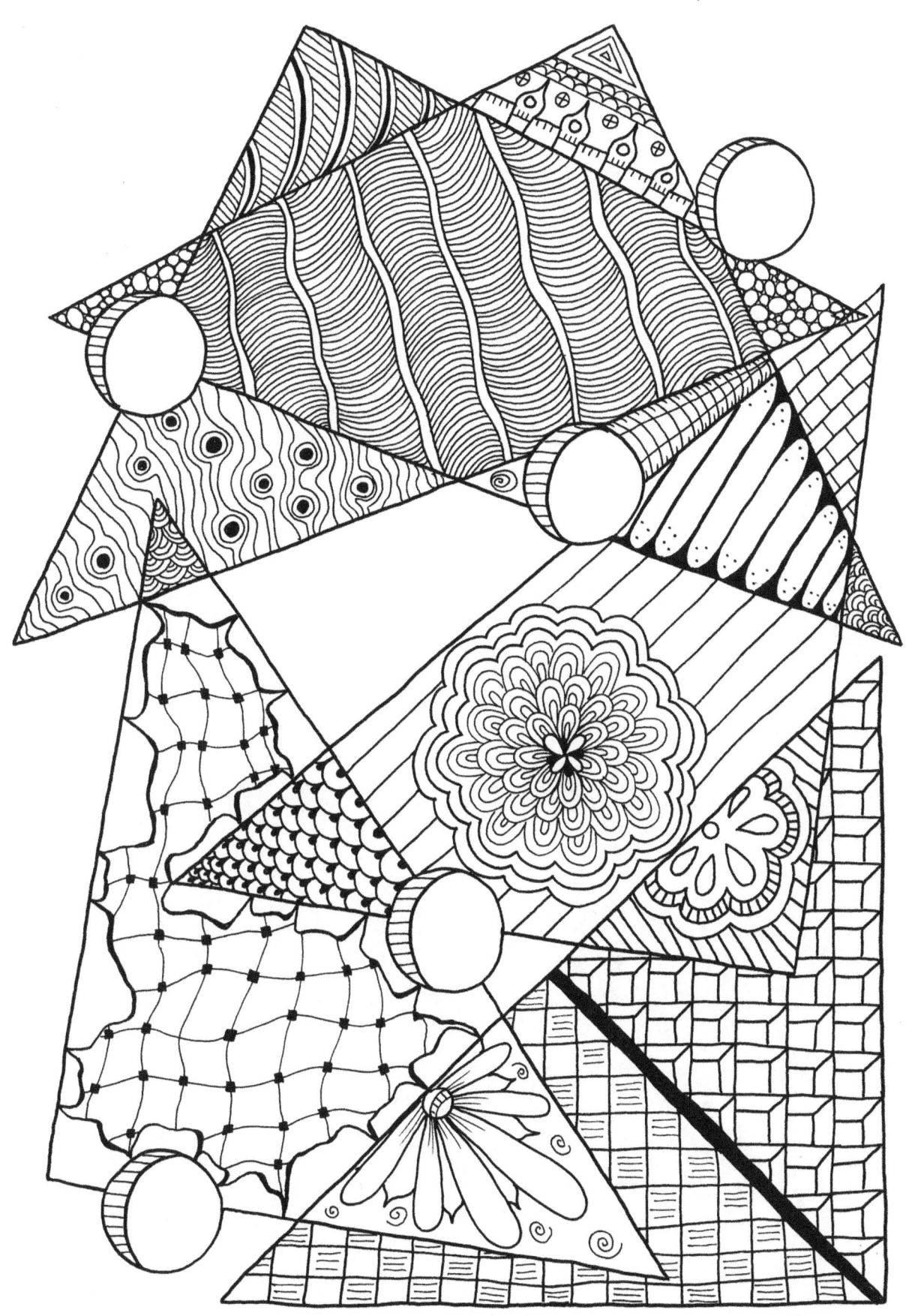

Positive thoughts attract positive events and people.
Negative thoughts attract negative events and people.

Change your thoughts, change your life!

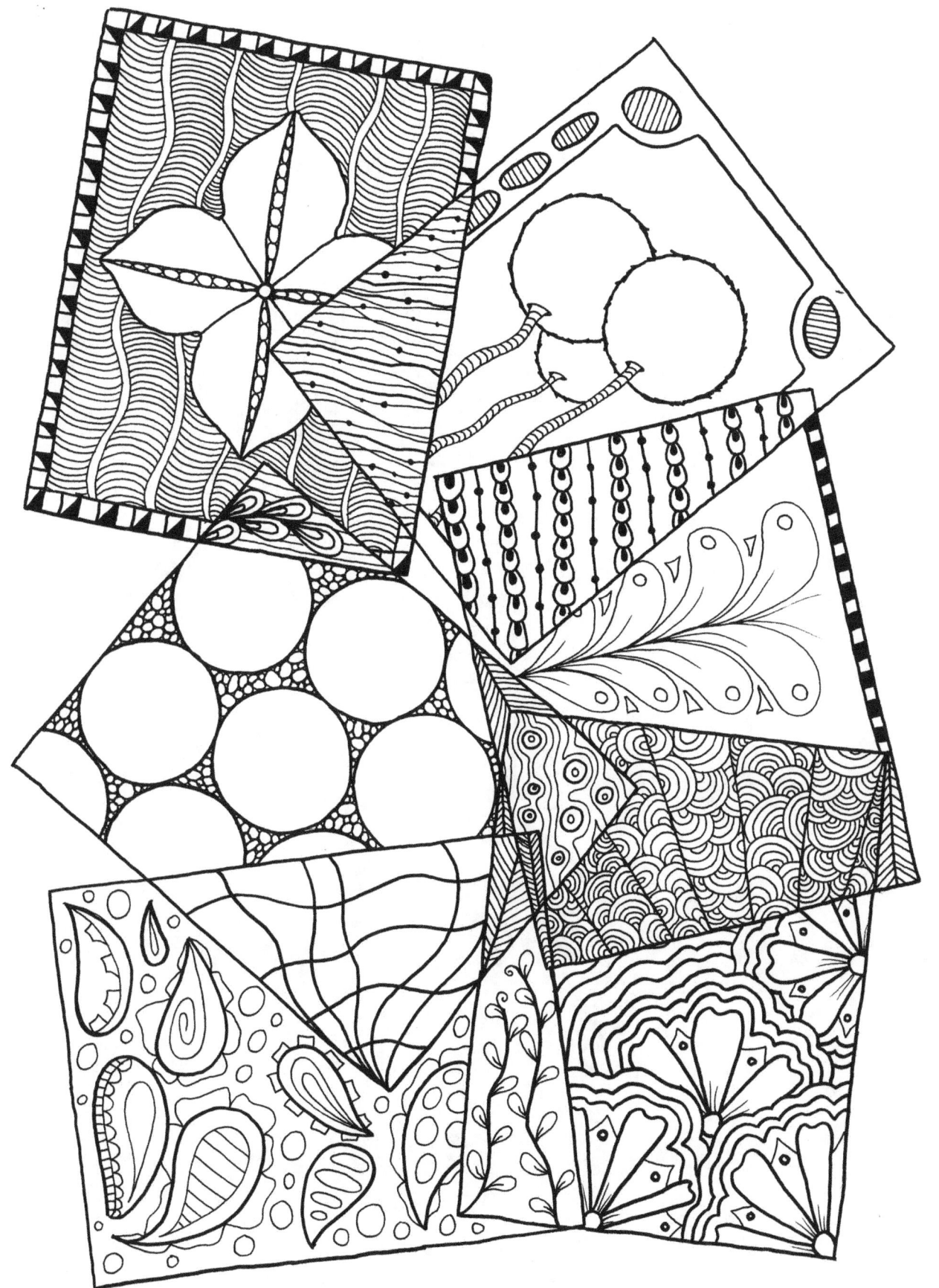

Stop worrying about what others think of you.
The only thing that matters is what YOU
think of YOU!

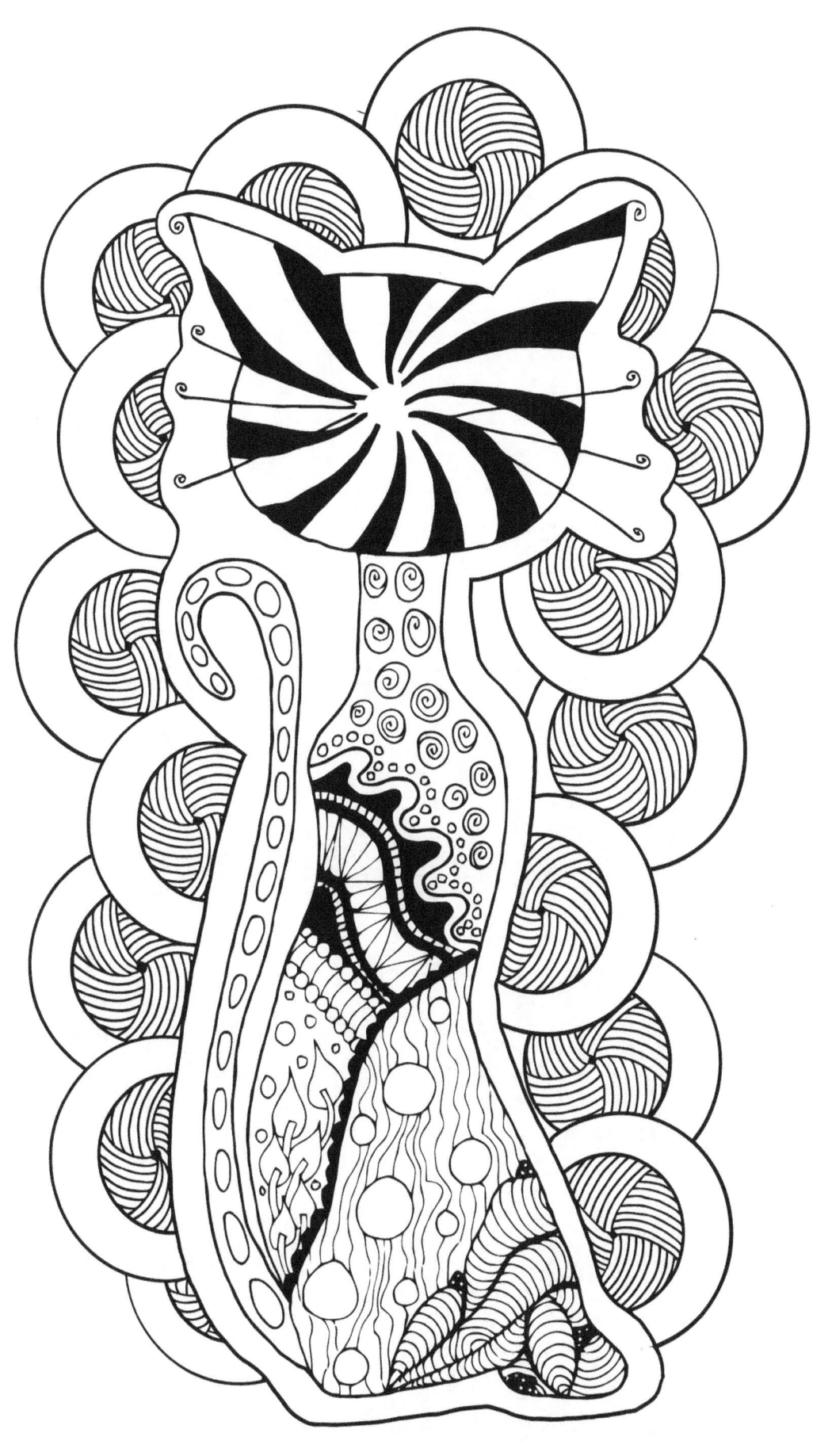

Some call it sticking my head in the sand.
I call it choosing to see the positive!

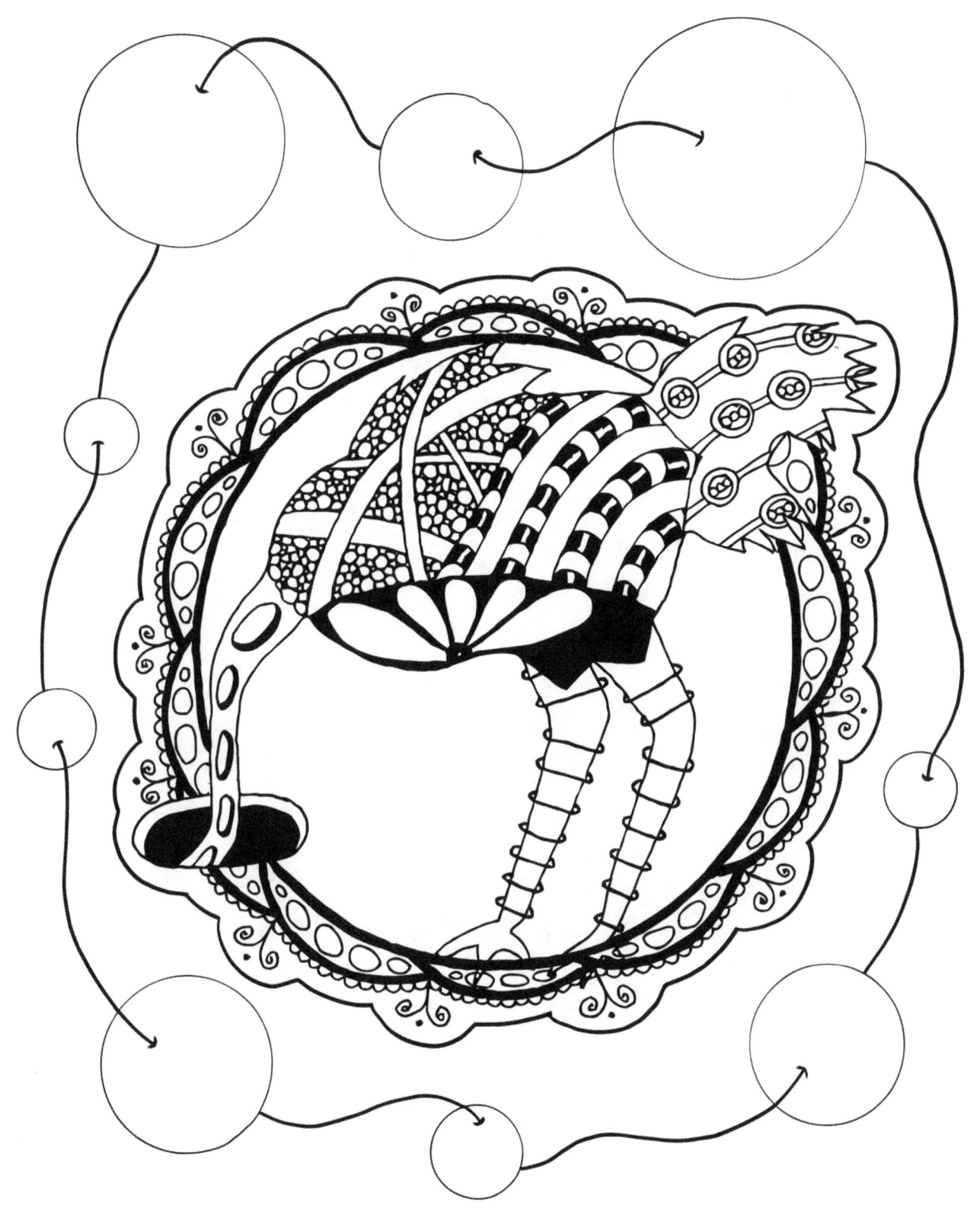

Good morning starshine
The earth says hello
You twinkle above us
We twinkle below
~ Hair

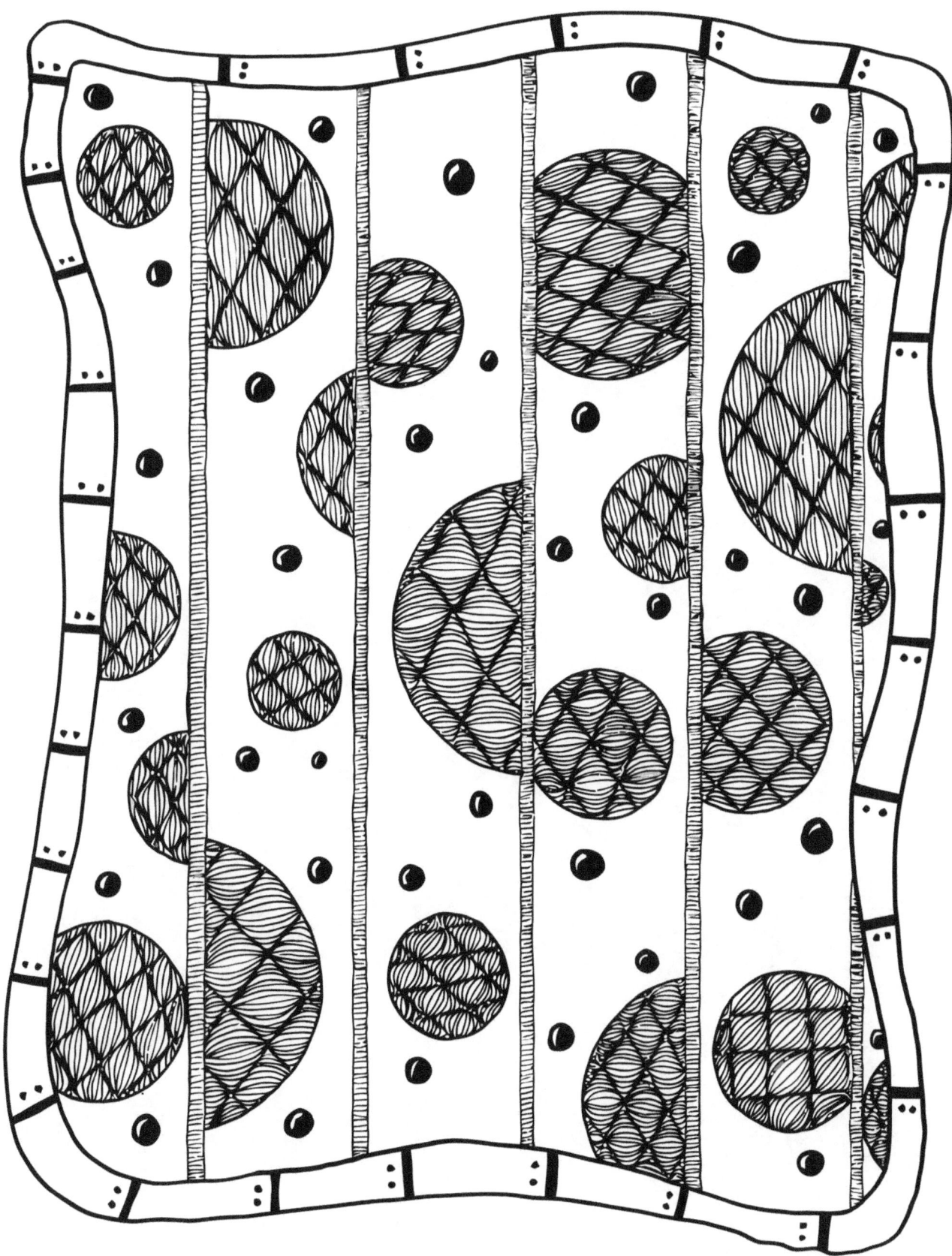

When in doubt, take the high road!

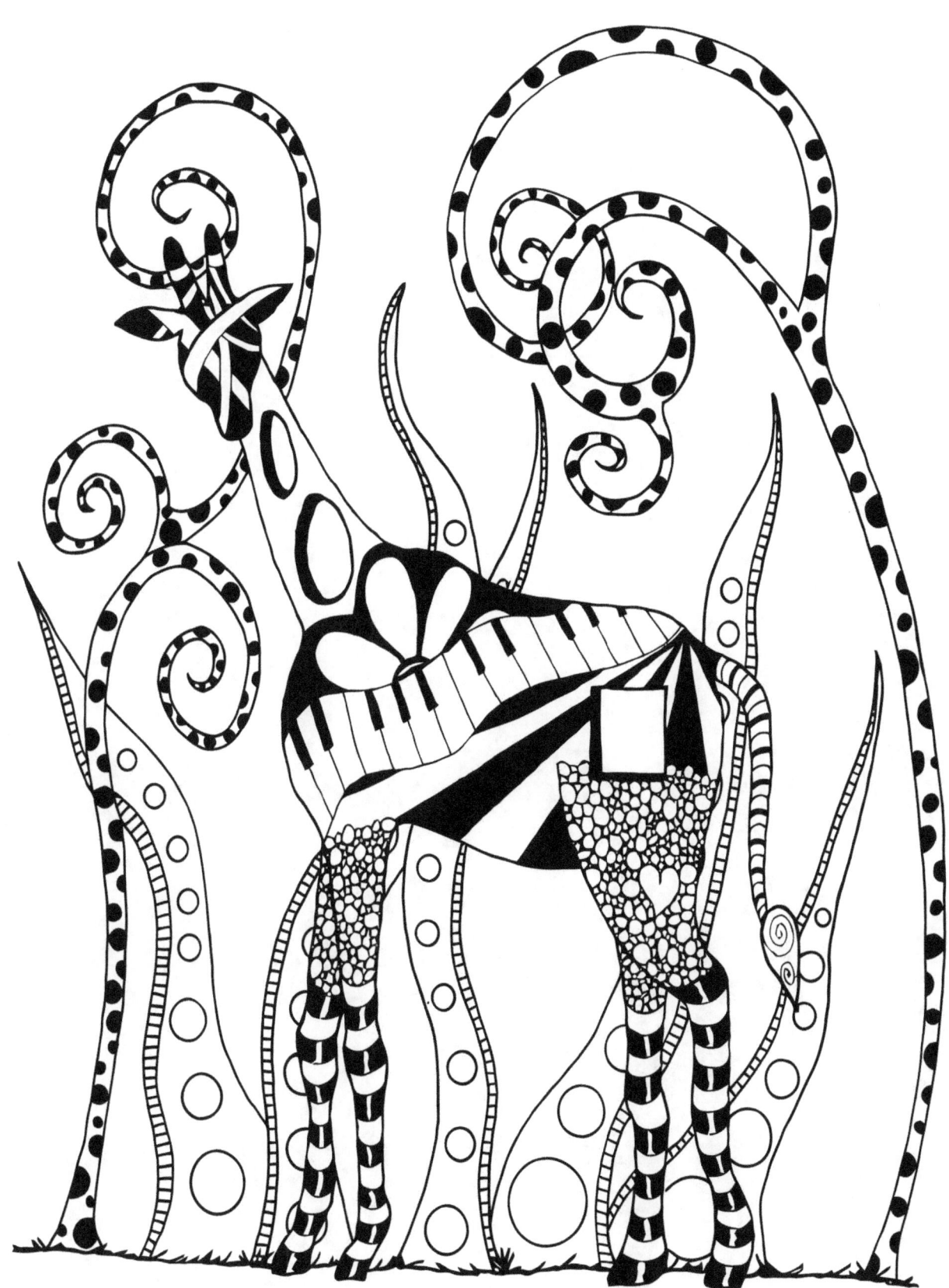

The zebra teaches us that sometimes blending into a crowd without losing your individuality is powerful.

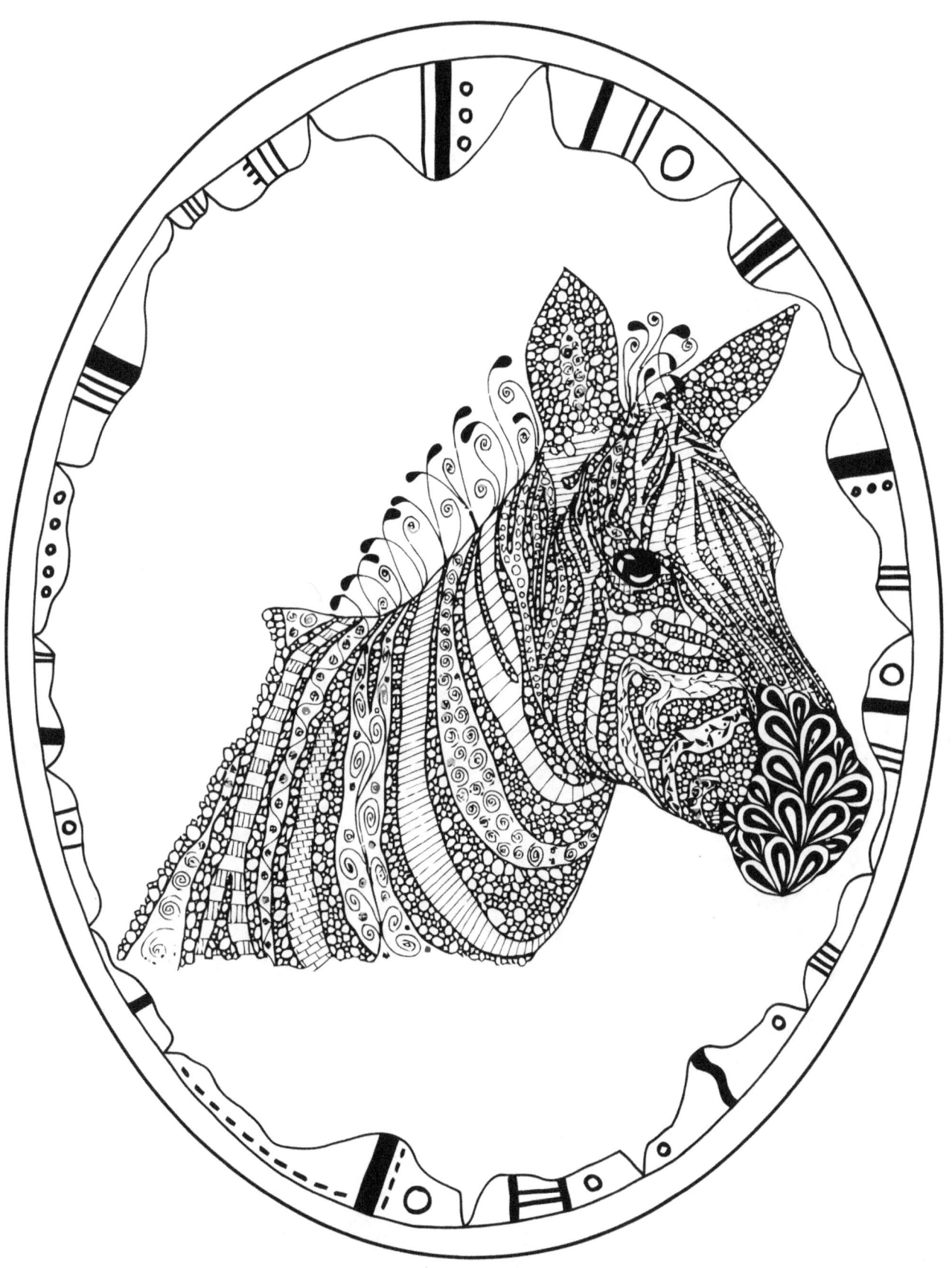

We are all connected.
We are all one.
Not one of us has more worth
more than the other.

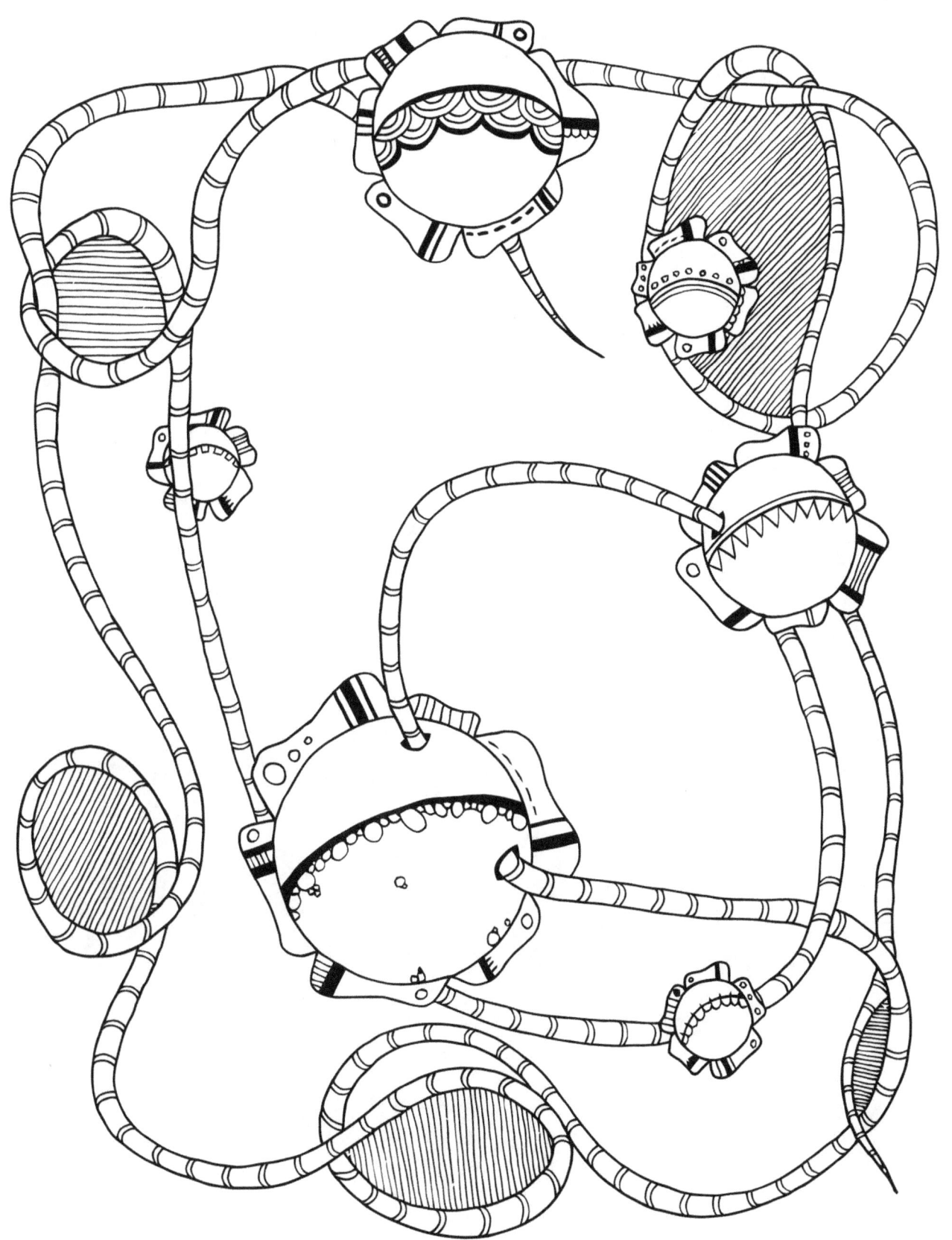

Hey, I'm a wildflower, growin' in the sunshine
Soakin' up the way of life I was raised in
Runnin' barefoot, bloomin' in a summer shower
Ponytail dancin', I can't help it, I'm a wildflower
~ The JaneDeer Girls

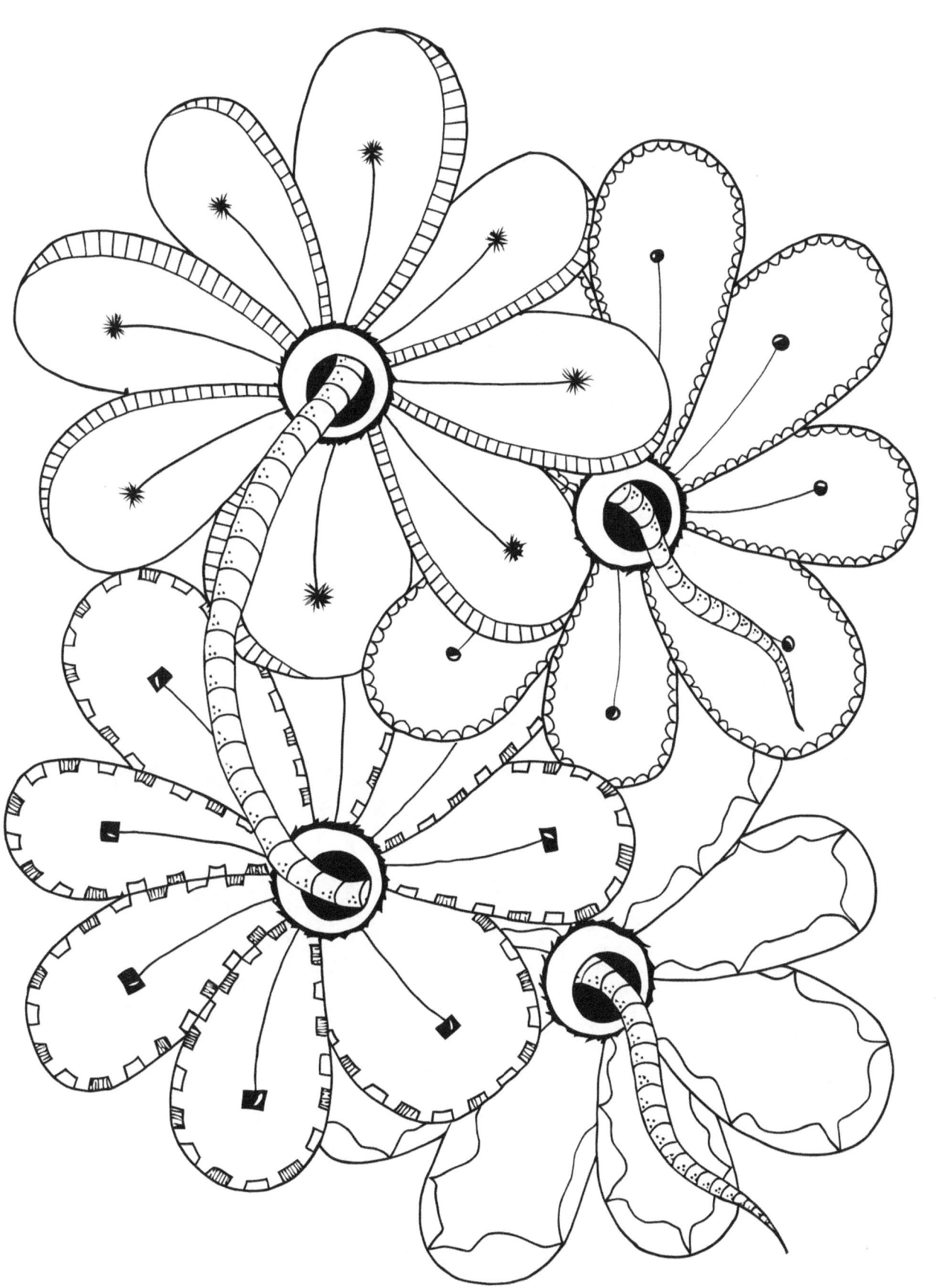

I need to laugh and when the sun is out
I've got something I can laugh about
I feel good in a special way
I'm in love and it's a sunny day
Good day sunshine
~Beatles

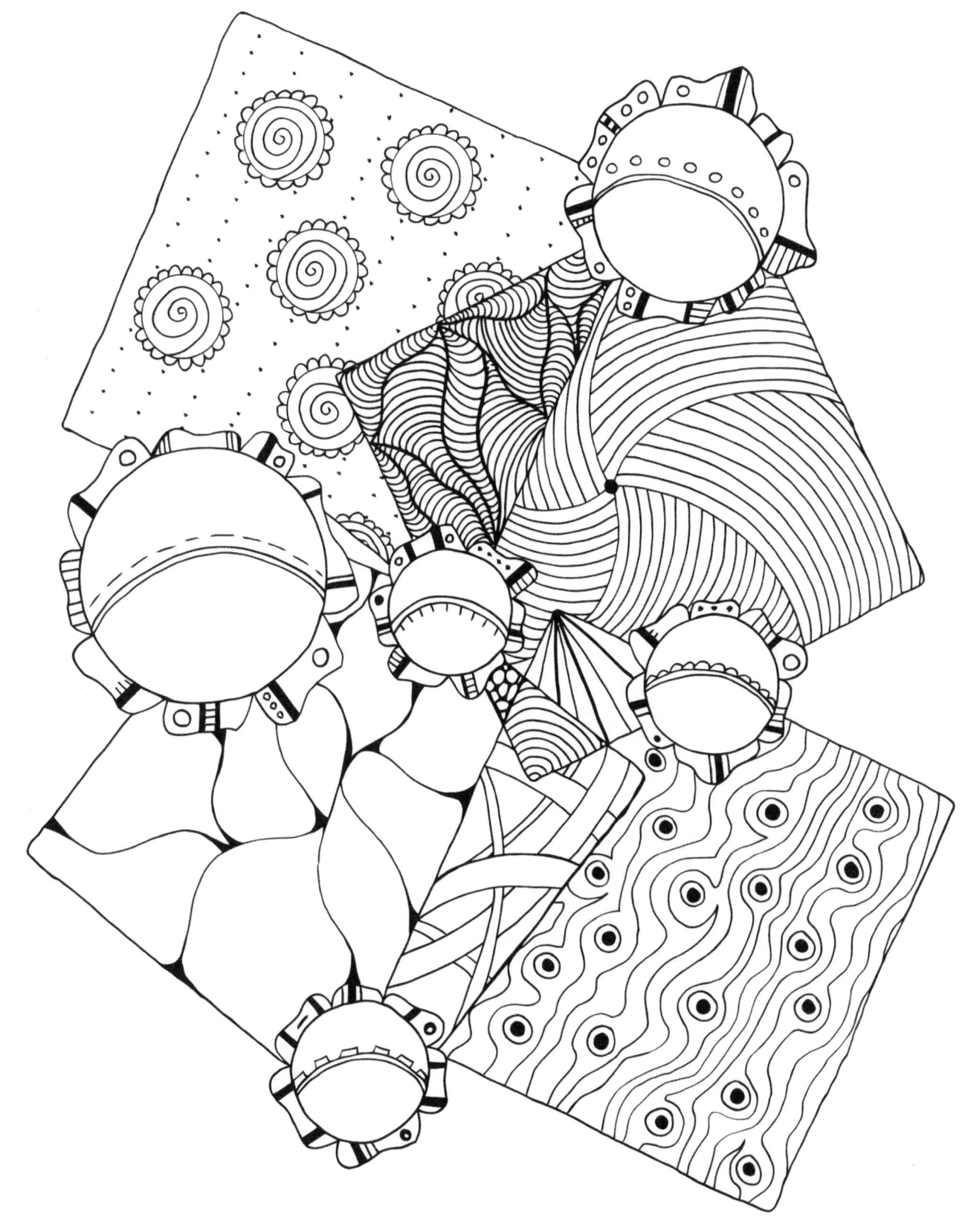

Sometimes it's best to brave the wind and rain
By havin' strength to go against the grain
~ Garth Brooks

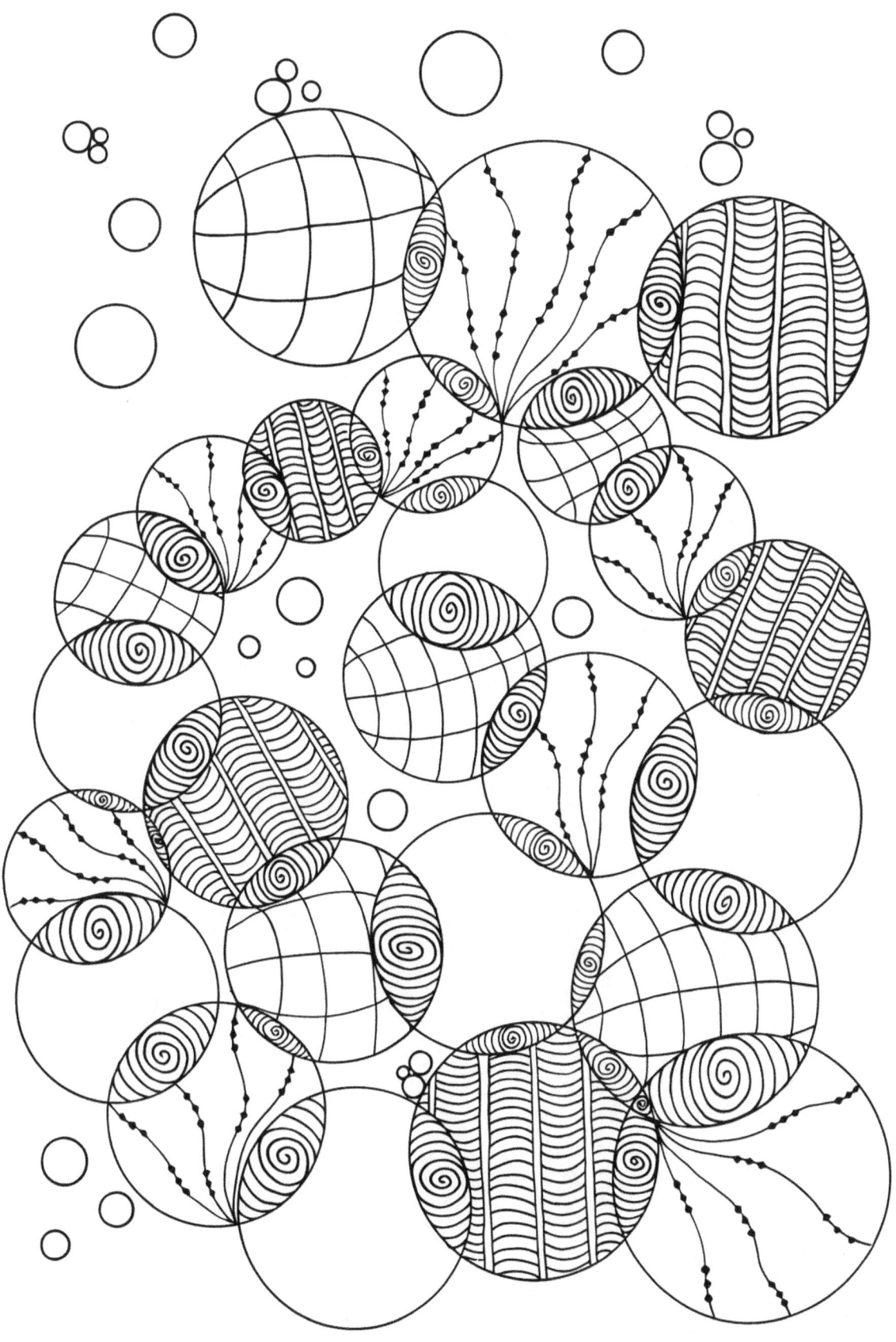

So I just let go of what I know I don't know
And I know I'll only do this by
Living in the moment
Living our life
Easy and breezy
With peace in my mind
With peace in my heart
Peace in my soul
Wherever I'm going, I'm already home
~ Jason Mraz

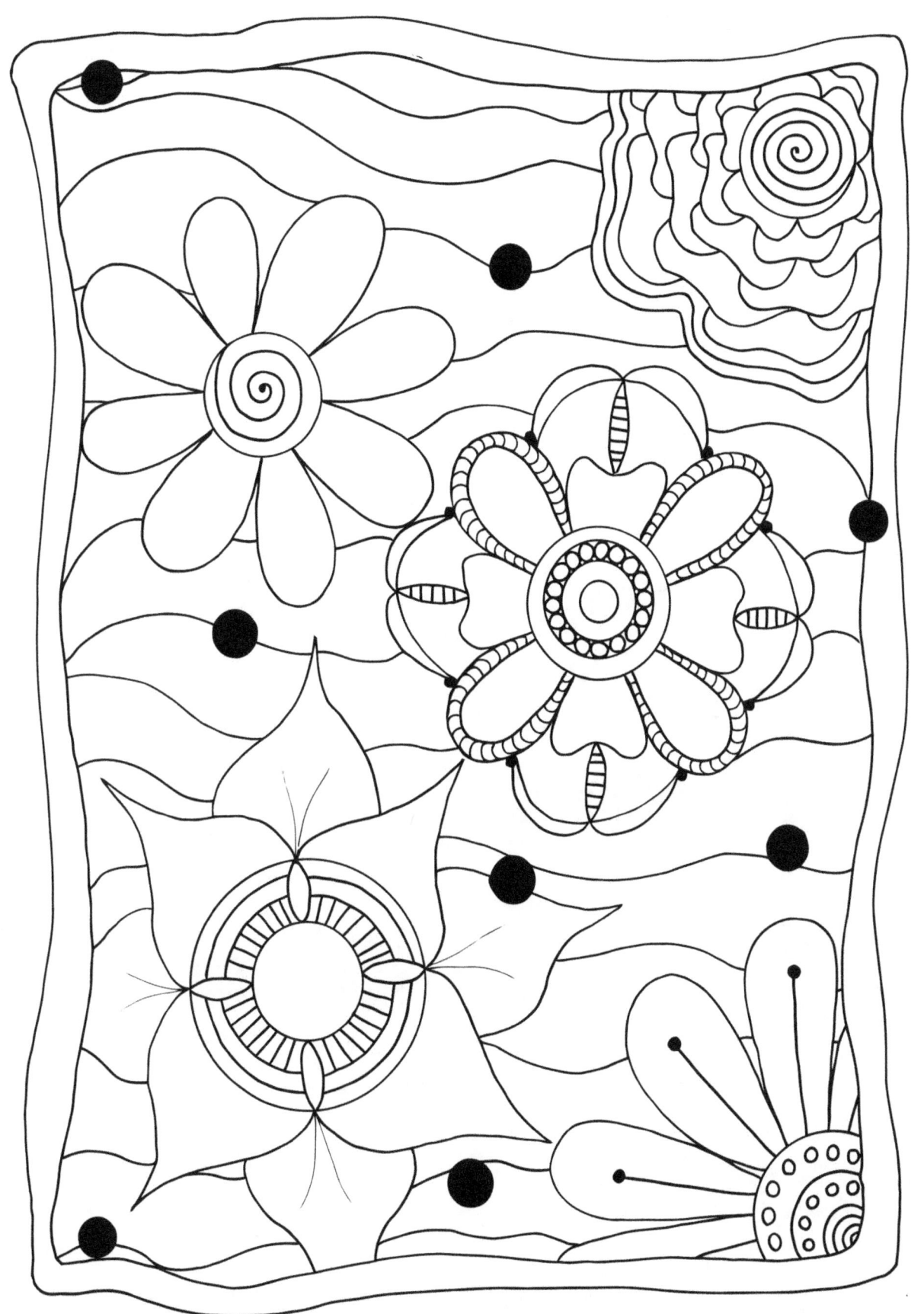

The moment you doubt whether you can fly,
you cease forever to be able to do it.
~ J.M. Barrie

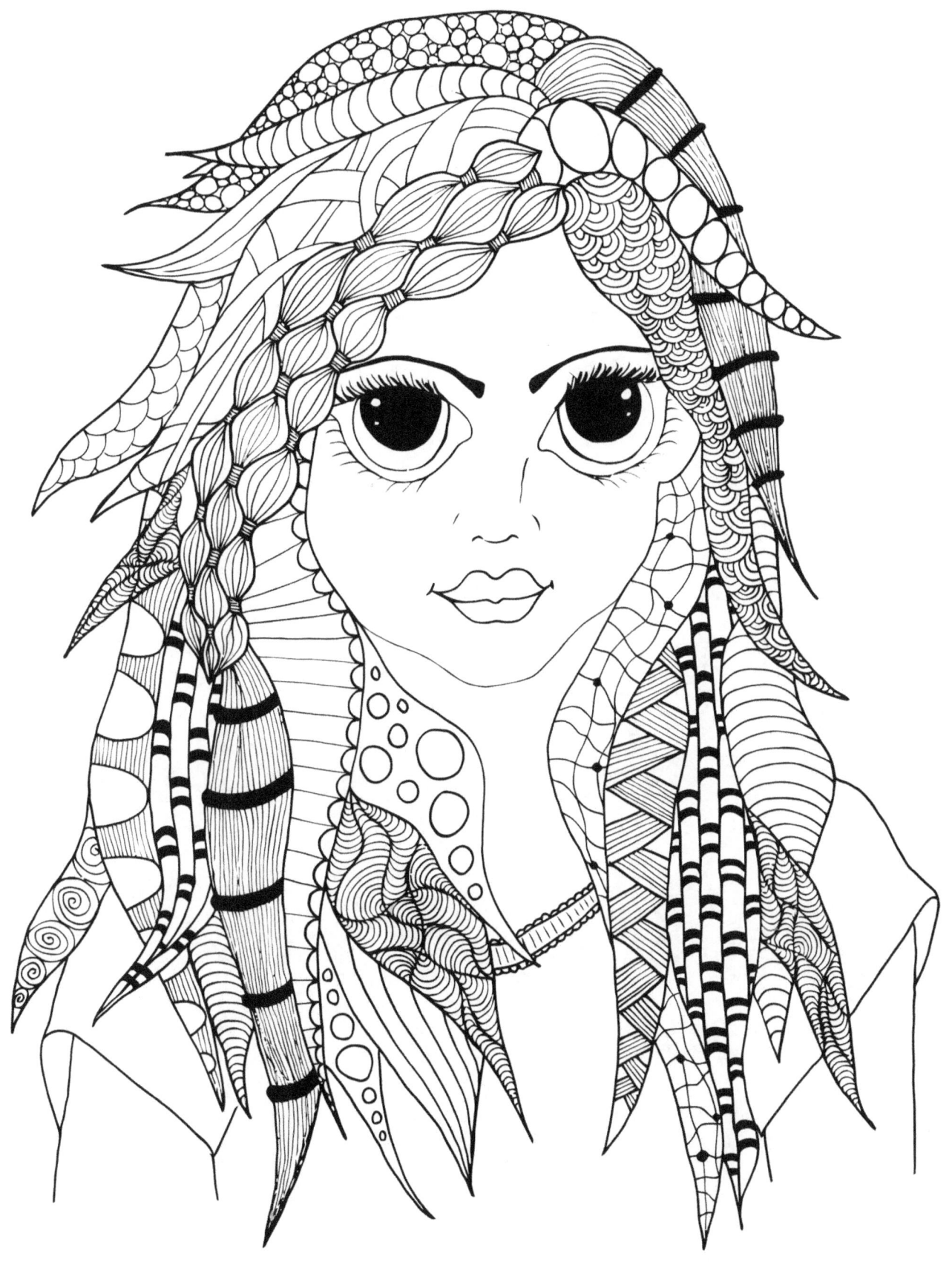

When you're different,
sometimes you don't see the millions
of people who accept you for what you are.
All you notice is the person who doesn't.
~ Jodi Picoult

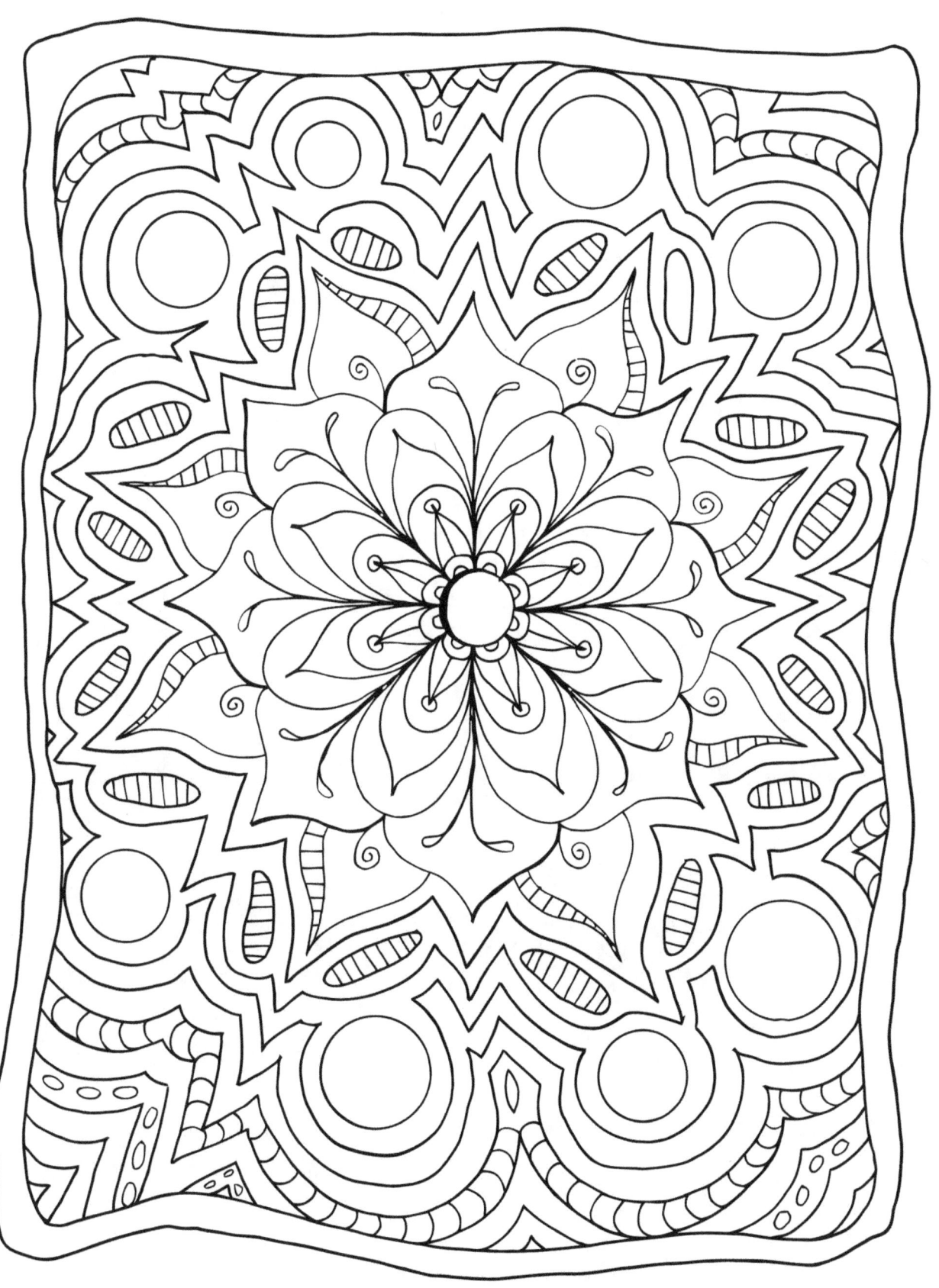

Life is ten percent what you experience
and ninety percent how you respond to it.
~ Dorothy M. Neddermeyer

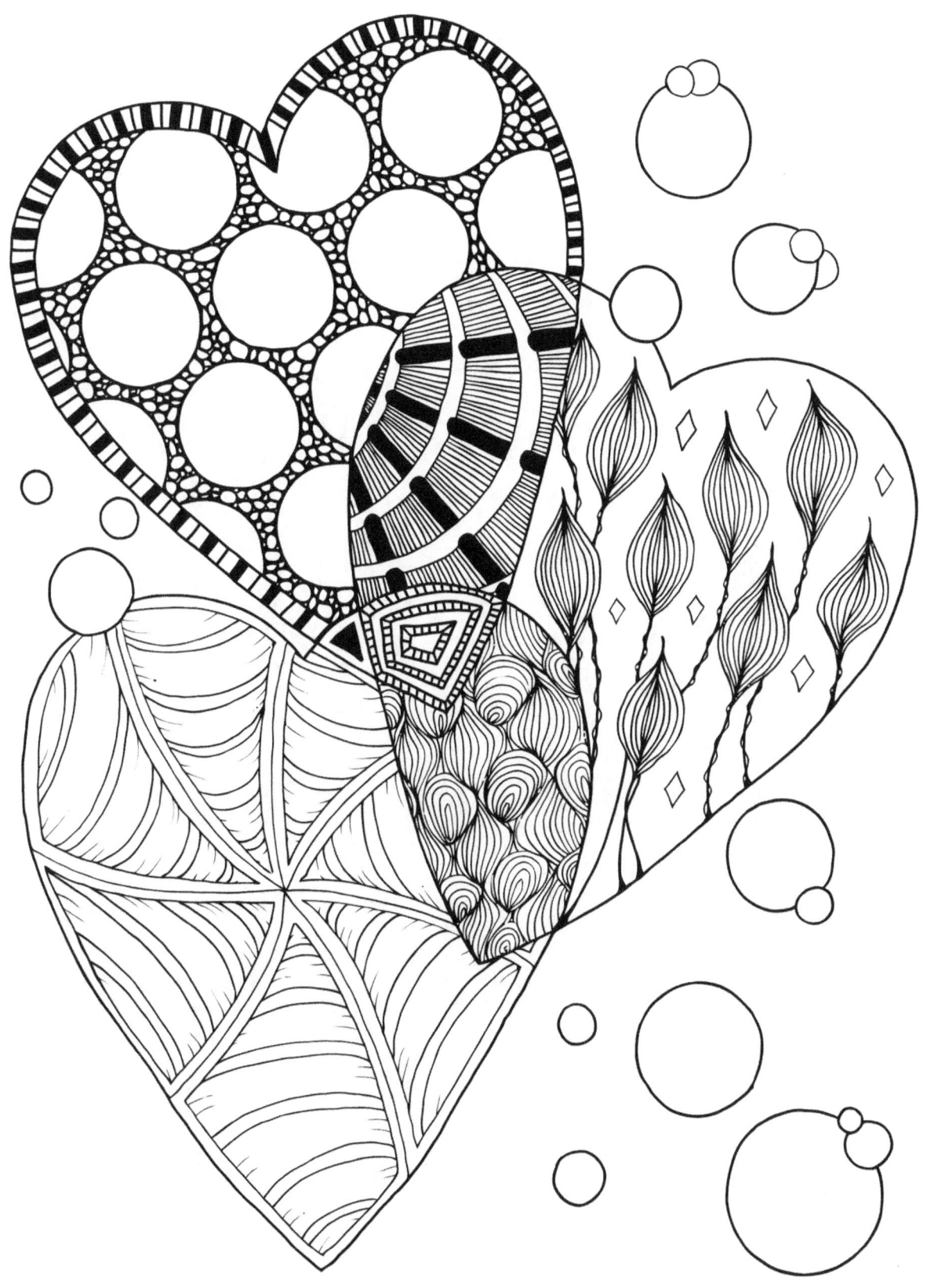

Knowing how to be solitary is central
to the art of loving. When we can be alone,
we can be with others without using them
as a means of escape.
~ Bell Hooks

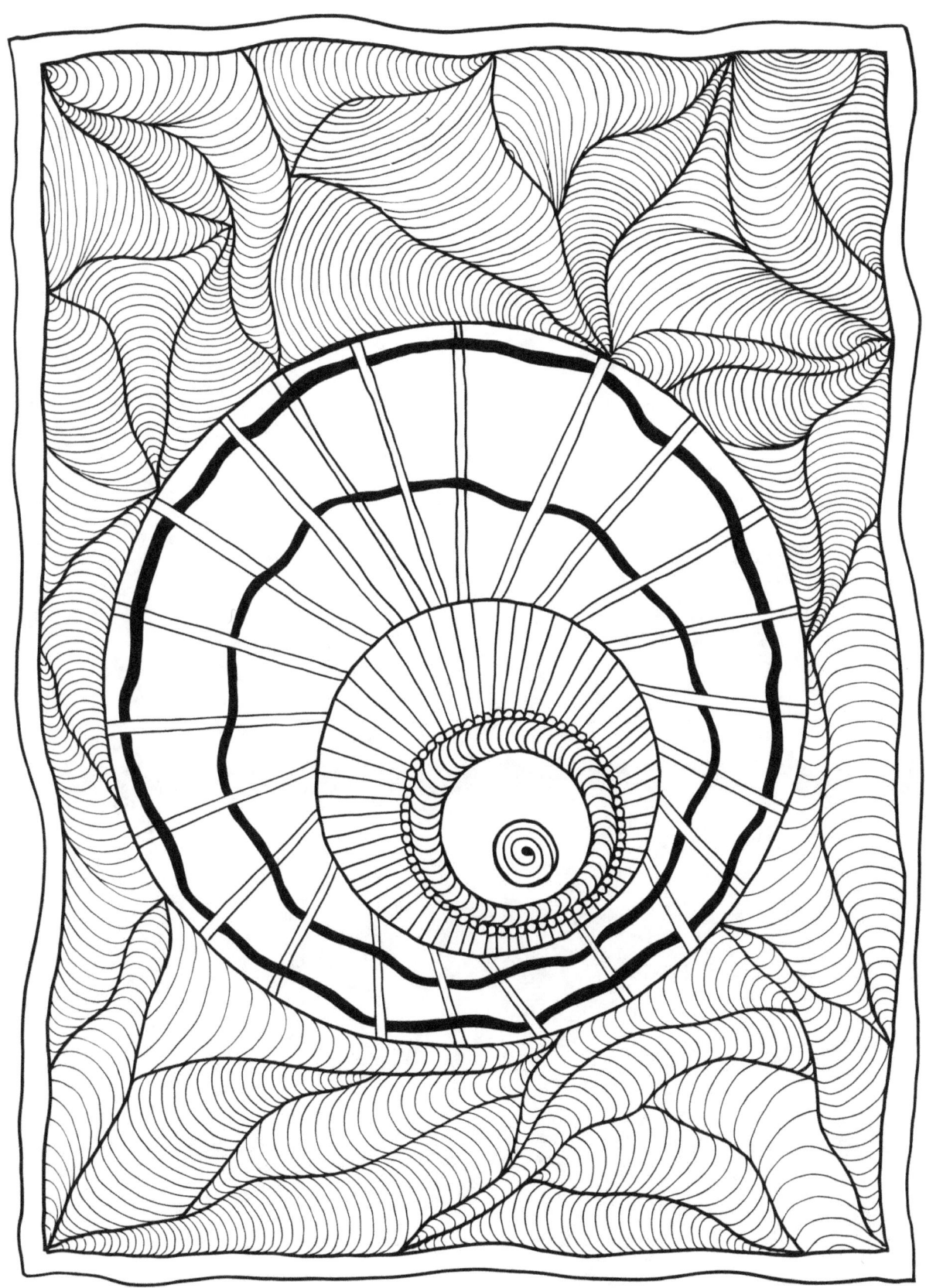

I would rather be damned by my honesty,
than caged by my lies.
~ Omega Maverick

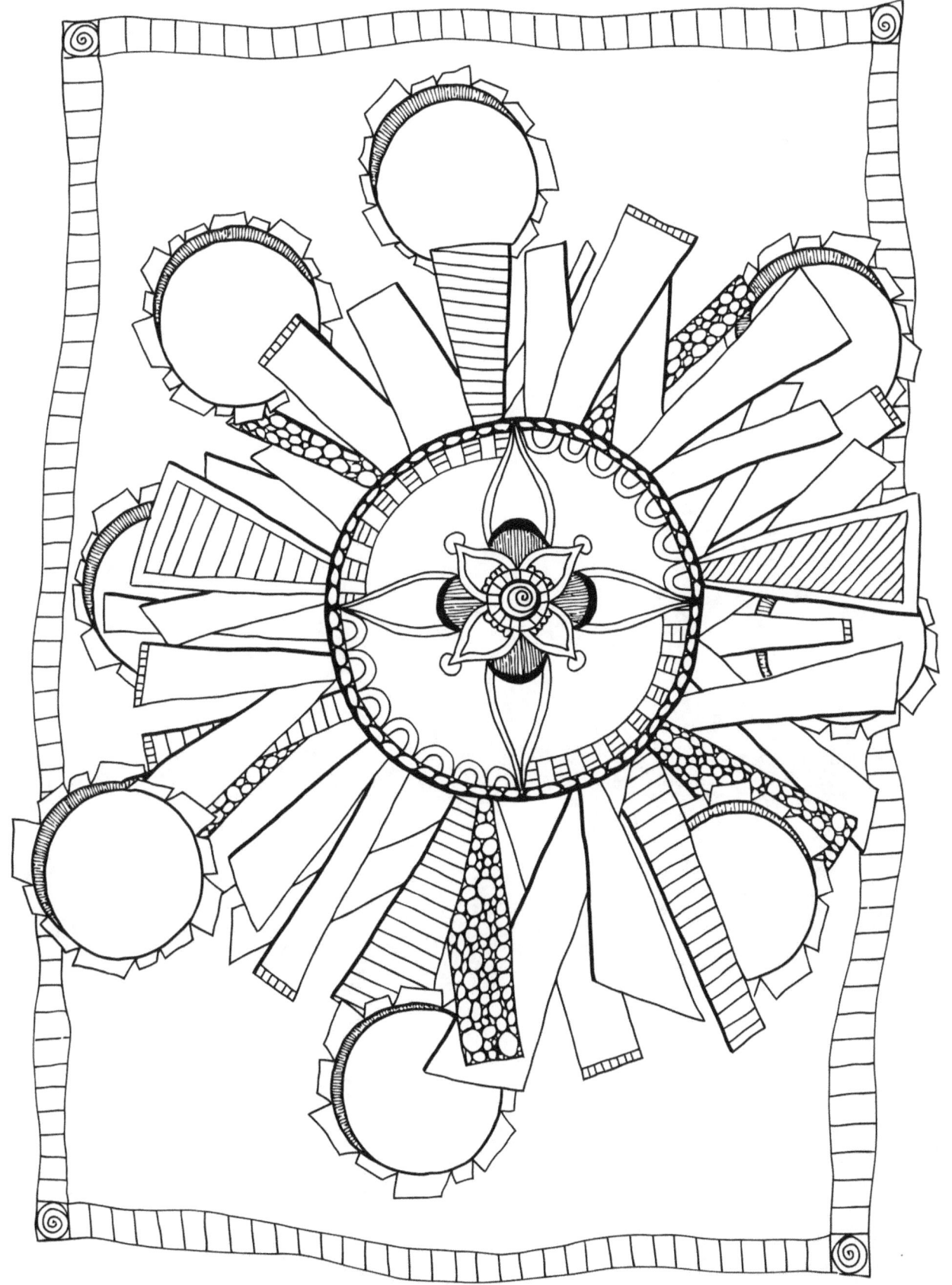

Keeping busy and making optimism a way of life
can restore your faith in yourself.
Lucille Ball

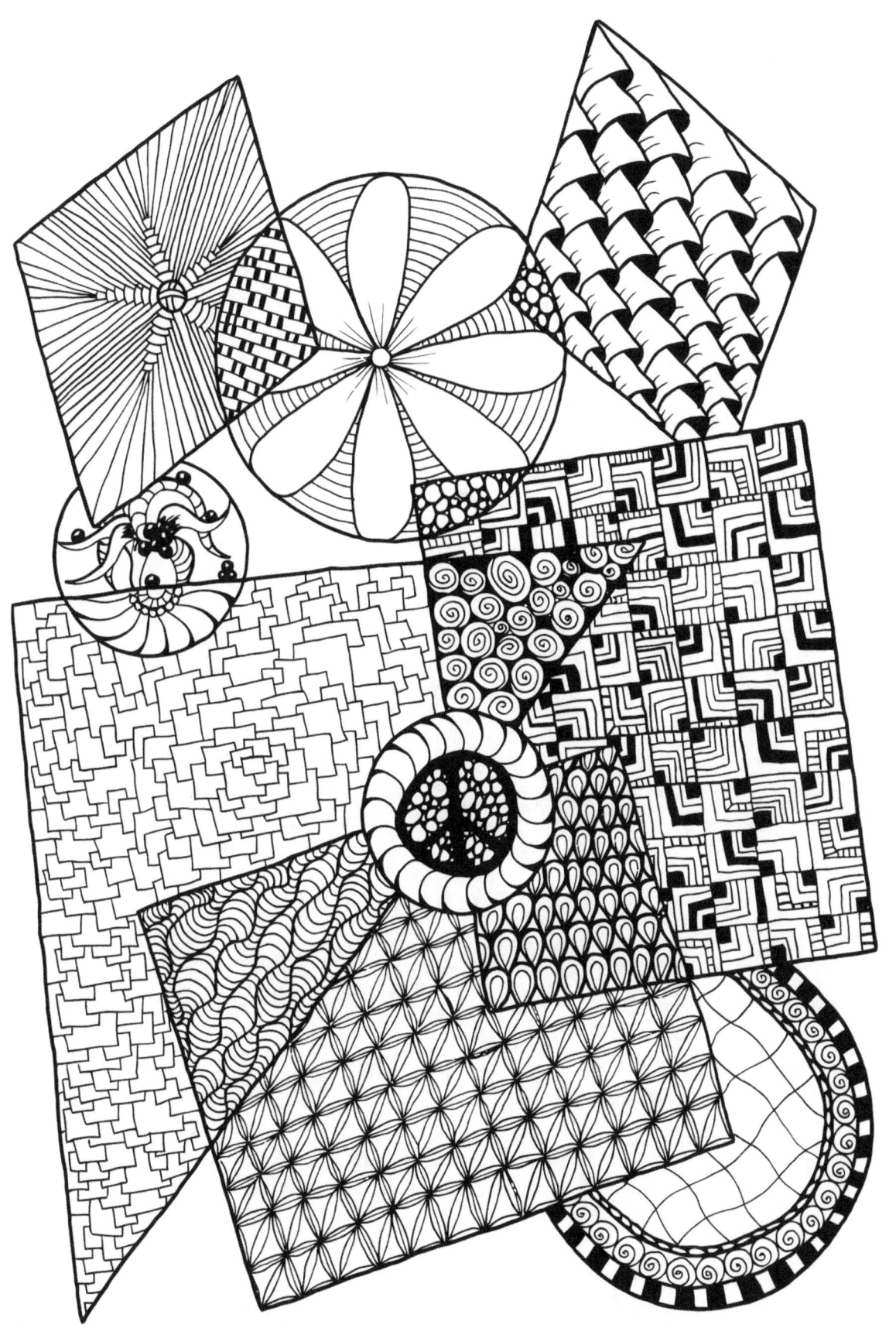

Fear defeats more people than
any other one thing in the world.
~ Ralph Waldo Emerson

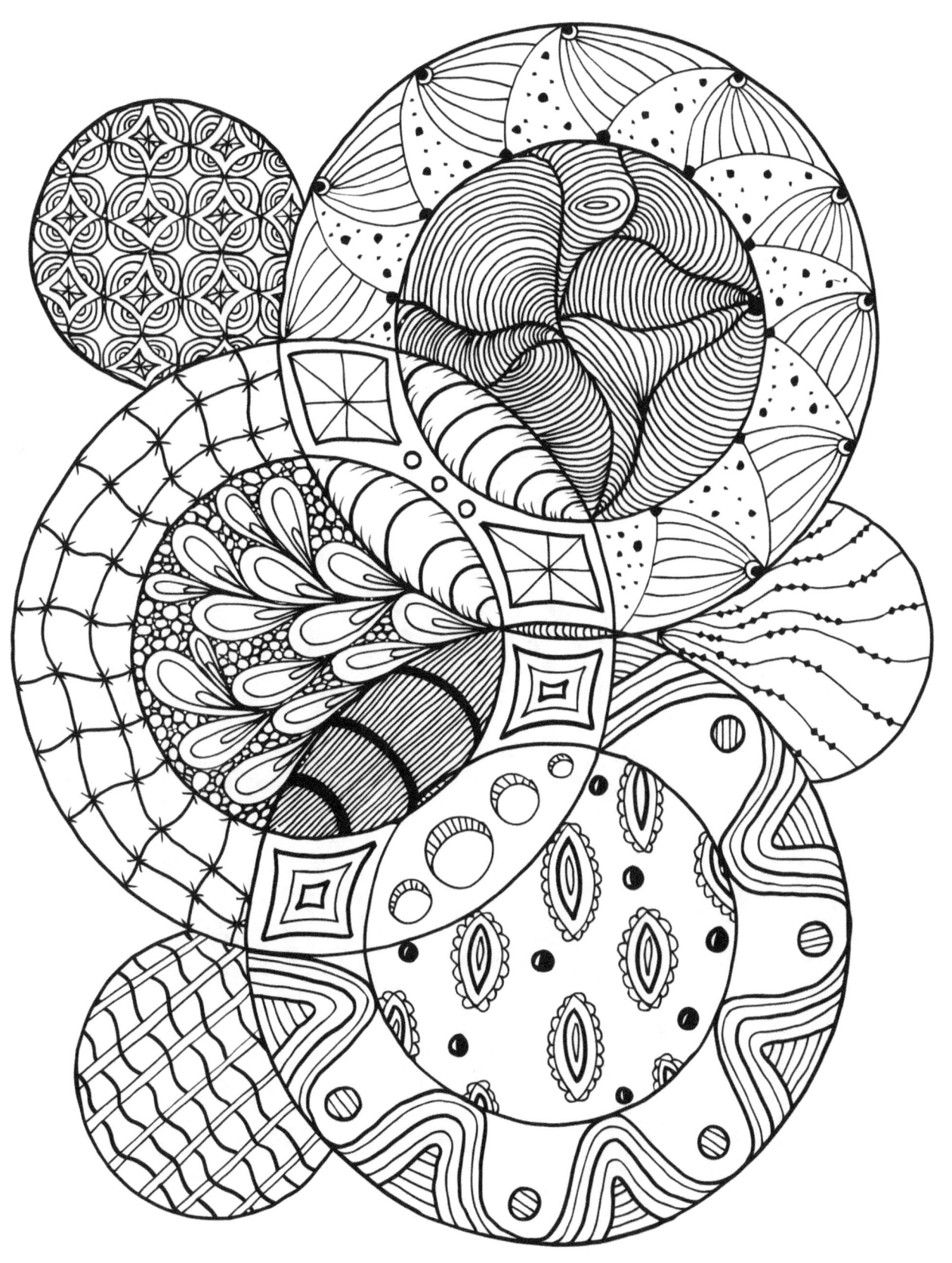

If you want a happy ending, that depends,
of course, on where you stop your story.
Orson Welles

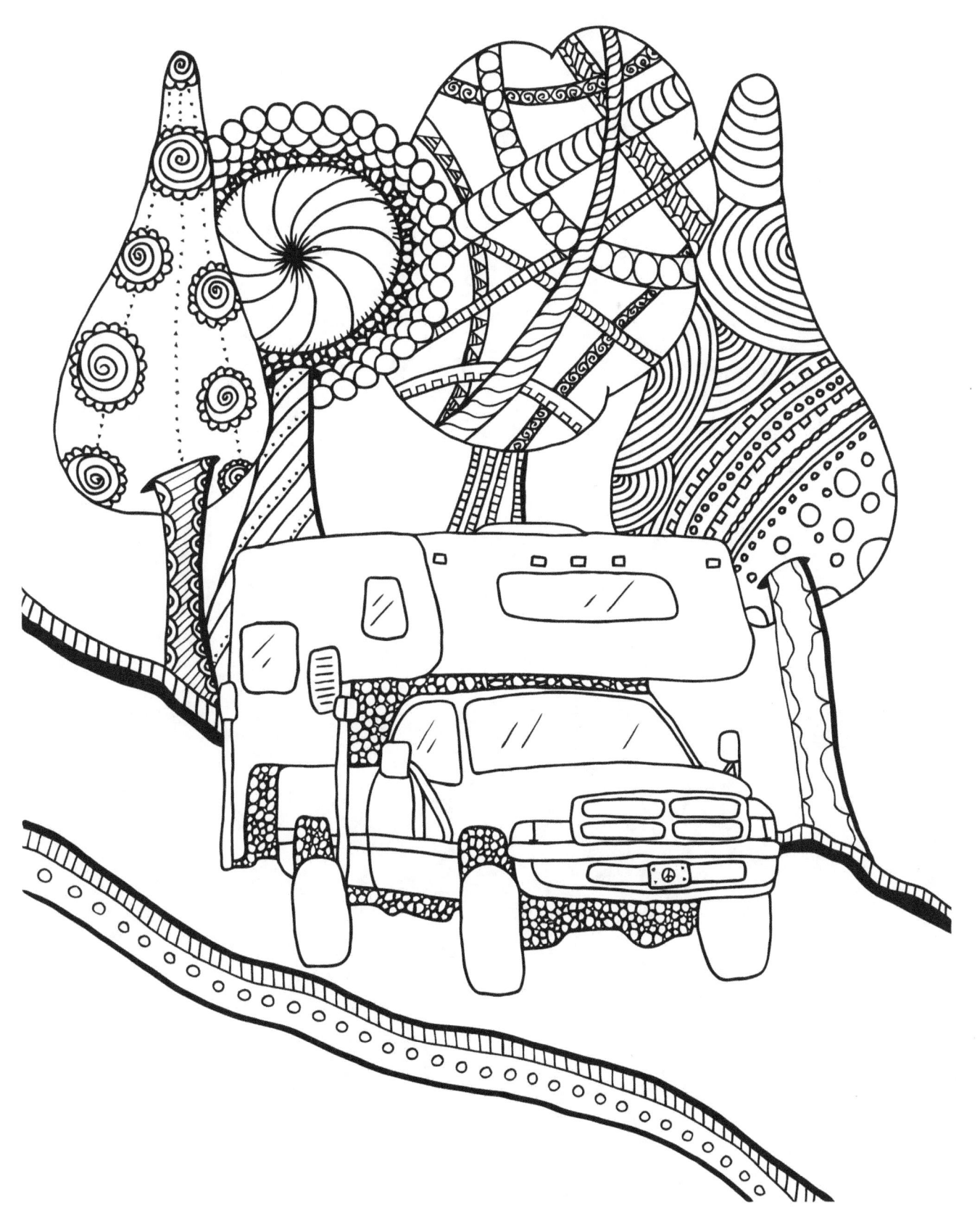

Would you like to create your own Zentangle-inspired art?

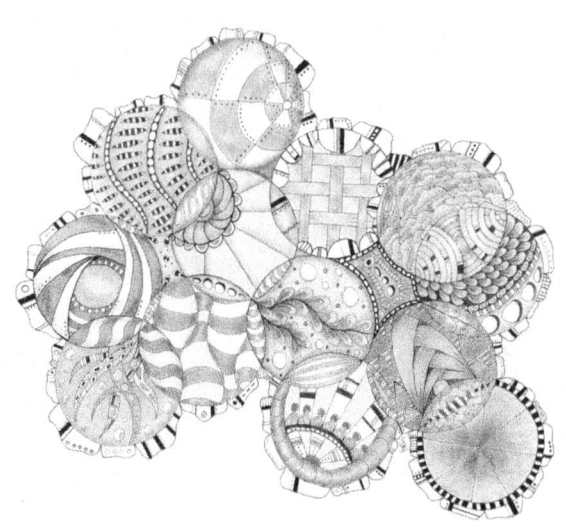

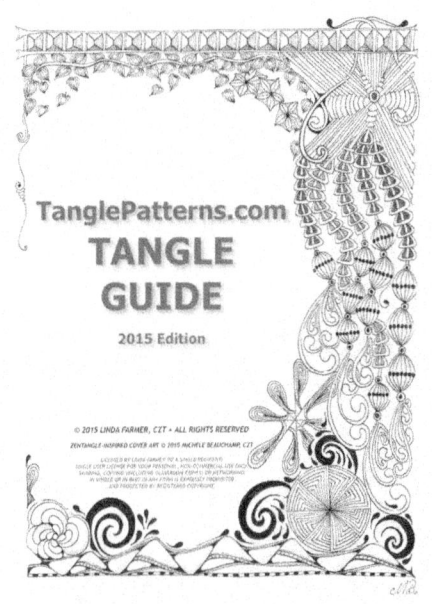

Linda Farmer, Certified Zentangle Teacher has created a fun website. It is an index and graphic guide to the best Zentangle® patterns on the web and how to draw them.
Visit it at tanglepatterns.com

The Zentangle® Method is an easy-to-learn, relaxing, and fun way to create beautiful images by drawing structured patterns. It was created by Rick Roberts and Maria Thomas. "Zentangle" is a registered trademark of Zentangle, Inc.

Learn more at zentangle.com.